D1710068

# SOIL

BY PAM WATTS

The **Child's World**®
childsworld.com

Published by The Child's World®
1980 Lookout Drive • Mankato, MN 56003-1705
800-599-READ • www.childsworld.com

Acknowledgments
The Child's World®: Mary Swensen, Publishing Director
Red Line Editorial: Editorial direction and production
The Design Lab: Design

Design Element: Simon Tang/Shutterstock Images
Photographs ©: Simon Tang/Shutterstock Images, cover
(top), 1 (top); Shutterstock Images, cover (bottom), 1
(bottom), 13, 14, 16, 23; Pavel Rodimov/iStockphoto,
5; Galyna Andrushko/Shutterstock Images, 6; Sergio
Delle Vedove, 7; iStockphoto, 8, 10 (left) 17, 20; Oleg
Mit/Shutterstock Images, 10 (right); Julie A. Felton/
Shutterstock Images, 15; Damian Herde/Shutterstock
Images, 18; Phil Augustavo/Shutterstock Images, 19

ISBN 9781503808065
LCCN 2015958148

Printed in the United States of America
Mankato, MN
June, 2016
PA02305

## ABOUT THE AUTHOR

Pam Watts studied physics and neuroscience at Wellesley College. She also has a master of fine arts degree in writing for children and young adults from the Vermont College of Fine Arts. Watts lives in the San Francisco Bay Area in California.

# CONTENTS

# CHAPTER 1

# Soil Everywhere

Imagine you are in a garden. You dig down into the earth. Then you touch the soil. Maybe it is dry and cracked. Or perhaps it is damp from morning rain. It contains grains of brown dirt. But there are other things in it, too. You see roots from plants. You notice little pieces of rock. A tiny bug crawls on top of the soil. Deeper down, an earthworm wriggles. These **organisms** make the soil their home.

Without soil, nothing could grow. Soil provides food for plants and insects. Those insects and plants feed larger animals. We rely on soil for the food we eat. Soil also stores water underground. It adds **nutrients** to our food and water. Soil helps living things survive. You can find soil nearly everywhere on Earth.

Soil forms Earth's top layer. You can find soil in the desert and at the bottom of the ocean. Soil is underneath the skyscrapers in large cities. But not all soil is the same. It can have various colors and textures. Soil is a mixture of many different substances. It contains **minerals** from

*In a garden, soil helps a variety of organisms survive.*

broken-up rocks. It also contains air, water, and plant matter. The mixture of these ingredients is what makes different types of soil.

*In some deserts, soil is dry and cracked.*

Soil is filled with tiny organisms. A fistful of soil has millions of them. Most of these organisms are much too small to see. But scientists can study them. They collect soil samples from different regions. Then they use microscopes to see the organisms up close. Special cameras and computer programs also help scientists study the soil.

Using their equipment, scientists learn the soil's past. Some tiny pieces of soil were once part of vast mountains. Analyzing soil can help scientists understand the history of an area. Learning about soil is useful for other people, too. Farmers' crops grow best in healthy soil. Gardeners rely on quality soil to nourish flowers. Soil is all around us. It is also an important part of our daily lives.

## SOIL AND FLOODS

Soil is made up of pieces or particles. Often, water filters through the cracks between the particles. Soil with tiny particles sometimes traps water, since the water cannot fit through the cracks. The trapped water can lead to muddy fields or flooding. Some places get a lot of snow in the winter. In the spring, the snow melts. If the melted snow cannot get through the soil, it stays near the surface. The melted snow floods the land.

# CHAPTER 2

# What Makes Soil?

**S**oil may contain many materials. But it is mostly made of tiny bits of rock. Rock is created through a series of natural processes. Some rocks form from magma. Others are made of plant or animal matter. The rock takes hundreds or thousands of years to form.

*Over thousands of years, mountain rock breaks down into soil.*

Then, over time, the rock breaks apart. Scientists call this process the **rock cycle**. The rock cycle explains how Earth changes.

The rocks around you may not seem to change very much. But over thousands of years, even massive mountains break down. Wind, rain, lightning, and ice all eat away at rock. This process is called **weathering**. Tiny bits of rock break apart. **Erosion** carries the bits of rock away. These tiny bits of rock gather together. Often, they combine with plant or animal matter. They become part of the soil. Each part affects the soil's traits.

Pieces of soil are called grains. The size of the particles in the soil's **parent rock** determines the size of the grains. Scientists sort soil textures into three main types. Clay is one type. It has small grains. Soil with a clay texture often feels sticky.

## THE OLD MAN OF THE MOUNTAIN

In New Hampshire, a rock formation looked like a man's face. People called it the Old Man of the Mountain. Writers in the 1800s described the formation. But the top part was too heavy. Cracks began to appear in the 1920s. In 2003, it suddenly collapsed. The Old Man is now rubble. Some bits of the rock have already become part of the soil.

Silt is another type of soil. It has medium-sized grains. Silt feels like flour. Sand is a third type. This type of soil has large grains. Sand feels gritty and sharp. Often, soil is a combination of these textures. Scientists use words such as "silty sand" to describe soil textures.

Basalt and granite are two common rocks. They are made of mineral particles. The particles that make up granite are big. The particles that make up basalt are small. When basalt breaks down, it forms smaller soil grains. Soil from basalt usually contains mostly clay and

SOIL TEXTURES

SANDY SOIL

SILTY SOIL

silt. Granite breaks down into larger grains of soil. It becomes sandy soil. The soil has minerals from its parent rock. For example, granite contains the mineral quartz. Soil made from granite will also contain quartz.

Other factors also affect soil's texture and traits. One important factor is **climate**. In hot areas with little rain, soil is dry and dusty. Few plants grow in the soil. In wetter areas, the soil is moist. More plants and tiny organisms can be found in this soil.

The shape of a landscape affects how soil forms. It forms most quickly in areas with mountains. Rain causes small pieces of rock to slide down the mountain slopes. The pieces gather in valleys or waterways. There, they become soil. Soil forms more slowly in flat areas.

After soil forms, it continues to change. Droughts and floods can affect its texture. Living things also change the soil. Plants, animals, and people can help soil stay healthy. Some of their activities can also damage the soil.

# CHAPTER 3

# Plants in Soil

In nature, plants need soil to survive. The soil supports their roots. Without soil, plants would blow away in the wind. The soil also protects their roots from the weather. It keeps them warm in the winter and cool in the summer.

Soil helps plants in other ways, too. It captures water and air. Plants need water for **photosynthesis**. This is how plants make food. Plants use air to break down sugar for energy. They also get valuable nutrients from the soil. These nutrients include nitrogen, phosphorus, and calcium.

Soil is very important for plants' growth. But plants are important to soil, too. Have you seen a plant growing in the cracks of a sidewalk? As the plant grows larger, it can make the cracks wider. The same thing happens in natural rocks. Some plants begin to grow through small cracks in rock. Then the roots expand. Trees and other large plants can break off pieces of the rock. The pieces become soil.

*During photosynthesis, plants use sunlight, water, nutrients, and air to make energy.*

Plants sometimes get nutrients from nearby rock. Tree roots might grow under a rocky surface. Mosses and lichens grow on top of rocks. All of these plants can extract, or take, nutrients from the rock. This extraction makes the rock weaker. As a result, it crumbles more easily. The rock becomes soil more quickly.

*Tree roots help keep soil in place. The trees get nutrients from the soil.*

Once soil is created, plants can protect it. Plant roots can hold soil in place. Leaves shelter the soil against rain. Without these protections, erosion would carry the soil away. Plants' roots also carry nutrients. They bring the nutrients up to the top of the soil. The plants help worms and insects get the nutrients they need.

When a plant dies, it becomes part of the soil. The plant decays, and its parts break down. The dead plant matter keeps the soil healthy. It releases nutrients into the soil. The nutrients keep organisms in the soil healthy, too.

## LAYERS OF SOIL

Different layers of soil have different traits. Scientists call the layers of soil in a certain area a **soil profile**. The top layer contains plant matter and dark-colored soil. The next layer is rich in nutrients. This layer is called topsoil. The third layer, subsoil, is light-colored. It often includes clay and minerals. Below all of the soil layers is a solid layer called bedrock.

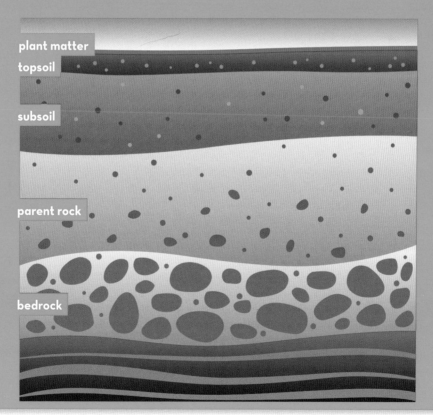

plant matter
topsoil
subsoil
parent rock
bedrock

# CHAPTER 4

# Animals and Microorganisms

**S**oil isn't only important to plants. It is also important to insects, animals, and other organisms. Millions of different **species** live in the soil.

*Ants dig tunnels in the soil. By breaking the soil down, they bring nutrients to the surface.*

Scientists keep track of the number of species. Healthy soil has many different species.

Without a variety of organisms, soil lacks nutrients. Plants have a hard time growing in it. The plants need nutrition from the soil. Animals need nutrition from plants. The more life there is in the soil, the more life it can support.

Some organisms, like earthworms, eat plants. They digest the plant material. Nutrients from the plant enter the soil through the earthworms' waste. Then, smaller organisms digest the soil. They get the nutrients they need.

Most of the organisms in soil are too small to see. The smallest ones are called microorganisms.

## HELP FROM EARTHWORMS

Earthworms are common in the United States. You might see them on sidewalks after a heavy rain. Earthworms live in soil. They keep the soil healthy. As they slither underground, they break down plant matter. They also leave holes in the soil. These holes can store rainwater. The earthworms help plants get the water they need.

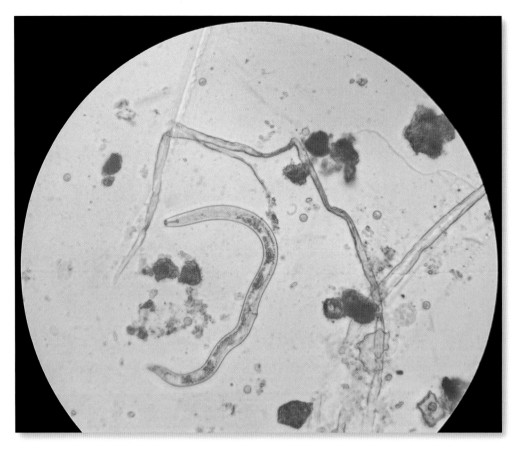

*Nematodes, shown through a microscope, are a type of microorganism that lives in soil.*

These tiny organisms break down dead plant matter. They help release nutrients from the plant matter into the soil.

Microorganisms, earthworms, and plants are all part of the soil food web. Each part of the web is important. Even the smallest creatures help the other species survive.

# CHAPTER 5

# People and Soil

**M**any natural processes affect soil. People affect the soil, too. Humans often speed up natural processes of creating and reducing soil.

In the mountains, people mine coal. They use tools to break apart mountains. It would take thousands of years for natural processes to break up the mountain rock. But people can do it in days. The mountain collapses into piles of rubble. The smallest pieces become soil. However, mining can also damage soil. Companies remove trees and plants from the land. **Deforestation** can cause

*Mining and deforestation can damage soil by causing erosion.*

*Farmers' choices can affect the quality of soil over time.*

erosion. Trees and other plants hold the soil in place. With the plants gone, wind or water can carry the soil away. It ends up at the bottom of waterways. Some erosion happens naturally. But natural erosion usually happens slowly. People can erode soil more quickly. This erosion can prevent plants from growing.

People have an effect on soil quality, too. Farming can reduce the number of organisms in soil. Often, farmers only plant one crop in a field. Focusing on one or two crops helps the farmers sell food. But it limits the nutrients in the soil. The soil can become unhealthy.

Farmers may also use insecticides. These substances make the soil less healthy over time. Adding fertilizer to the soil can add nutrients. Fertilizer helps the soil produce more crops. But scientists do not know the long-term effects of fertilizer on soil. Some fertilizers can harm wildlife.

There are some ways that people can improve soil. One way is to keep the ground covered. Wind, water, and other forces erode bare soil. A cover crop keeps the soil in place. Farmers can plant cover crops in between their main crops. Gardeners can plant cover crops around their flowers. Another way is to have soil tested. Scientists can analyze the substances in the soil. Then farmers can add nutrients to make the soil healthier.

Soil is very important to life on Earth. People, animals, and plants all rely on soil. Improving soil quality is a good way to help Earth.

## NO-TILL FARMING

Soil supports a variety of organisms. Moving the soil can harm the organisms that live in it. Some farmers try to avoid disturbing the soil. One technique is called no-till farming. No-till farmers do not plow their fields. They use special equipment to plant and harvest crops. The equipment helps prevent erosion of the soil.

# GLOSSARY

**climate** *(KLYE-mit)* Climate is the usual weather in a place. The climate of an area can affect its soil.

**deforestation** *(de-fawr-es-TAY-shun)* Deforestation is the cutting down of large areas of trees. Deforestation can harm soil.

**erosion** *(i-ROH-zhuhn)* During erosion, bits of worn rock are carried away by water or wind. Erosion breaks down rocks into smaller particles.

**minerals** *(MIN-ur-uhlz)* Minerals are substances found in nature that are not animals or plants. A rock may contain many minerals.

**nutrients** *(NOO-tree-unts)* Nutrients are substances that give organisms what they need to survive. Many plants and animals rely on nutrients in soil.

**organisms** *(OR-guh-niz-umz)* Organisms are living things. Soil contains organisms such as plants, worms, and insects.

**parent rock** *(PAIR-unt ROK)* Soil forms from parent rock. The type of parent rock affects the traits of the soil.

**photosynthesis** *(foh-toh-SIN-thuh-sis)* Photosynthesis is the process plants use to make food. Sunlight, water, and nutrients are necessary for photosynthesis.

**rock cycle** *(ROK SIGH-kul)* The rock cycle is the process of rocks forming and breaking down over time. Soil is an important part of the rock cycle.

**soil profile** *(SOYL PROH-file)* The layers of soil in a particular area are a soil profile. Often, the top layers of a soil profile include plant leaves and roots.

**species** *(SPEE-sheez)* Species are specific groups of living things that share common traits. Soil contains many different species of plants and animals.

**weathering** *(WETH-ur-ing)* Weathering is a natural process that wears down rock. Over time, weathering happens to all rocks.

# TO LEARN MORE

## IN THE LIBRARY

Barker, David. *Soil*. Ann Arbor, MI: Cherry Lake Publishing, 2011.

Dee, Willa. *Erosion and Weathering*. New York: PowerKids, 2014.

Tomecek, Steve. *Dirt*. Washington, DC: National Geographic, 2007.

## ON THE WEB

Visit our Web site for links about soil: **childsworld.com/links**

*Note to Parents, Teachers, and Librarians: We routinely verify our Web links to make sure they are safe and active sites. So encourage your readers to check them out!*

# INDEX